PHOTOGRAHY FOR BEGINNERS

PRONOB NARAYAN DEKA

ISBN 978-1-63957-073-7

Contents

INTRODUCTION

If you enjoy traditional photography and are still fairly new to digital media, this is the right choice for you. In this book you will find basic information about the types, components, and concepts as well as the pros and cons of using your digital camera.

The book will introduce the basics techniques of Photography. The book deals with the basic steps in taking a good photograph. People will also learn the different types of photography.

People take photos for numerous reasons. Some take pictures for scientific reason while others shoot to document the events of the world. Some take pictures for a live advertising and many do it for enjoyment and artistry.

The book also focuses of the various types of photography camera, lenses and the various tools. People will learn the art of taking a good picture and how to convert it to a masterpiece.

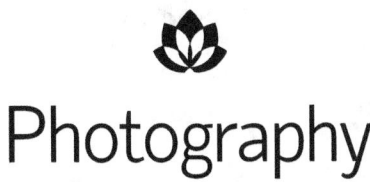

CHAPTER ONE

Photography

Brief History of Photography

Long before photography was discovered, artist used a cameras dark chamber or obscure in Italian. Light would enter the chamber through a small opening called a pinhole and the light would then project an image of the scene on to the opposite wall. At first, large rooms were specially designed to exhibit this "magical" phenomenon; but in the 16th century, Italian artists compressed the size of the chamber to a portable box, replaced the pinhole with a lens, added a mirror to invert the image, and a translucent glass panel to display it. They manually traced the projected image by hand. Henry Fox Talbot as well as others had the idea to capture and reproduce the image directly and this led to the birth of photography. Despite the drastic changes in technology over the years, the dark box and the lens still form the foundation of modern photography.

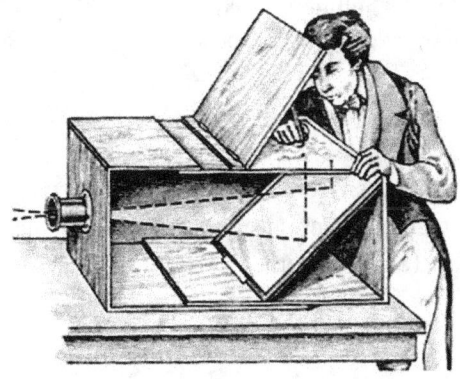

Introduction to Digital Photography

Traditional film photography uses a chemical process to expose and capture images. The camera lens and body allow a prescribed amount of light to come into contact with the film, which is basically a sheet of plastic that has been coated with a light sensitive chemical compound. Once the film is sufficiently exposed to light an invisible picture is formed. When the film is developed, other chemicals are applied and the image then becomes perceptible forming a negative image which then can be enlarged and printed on photographic paper.

In digital photography the film is replaced with a light sensitive electronic device known as an image sensor. These sensors are made up of millions of photoelectric devices that convert light into an electrical signal. The two most common types of image sensors used in digital cameras are CCD (charge coupled device) and CMOS (complementary metal-oxide semiconductor) sensors.

The strength of the electrical signal depends upon the amount of the light that exposes the image sensor. These electrical signals are then processed through a series of complex electronic circuits and finally stored in some type of internal or external flash memory in a standard image file format such as a JPEG file. (JPEG = Joint Photographic Experts Group). When processed by a computer, these files produce an image which is able to be printed on photographic paper.

Just as camera film is available in different sizes so are digital image sensors. The smaller sensors found in cell phone cameras and small point and shoot cameras generally produces lower quality images than a larger sensor that would be found in a digital single lens reflex (SLR) camera.

CHAPTER TWO

Types of Camera And Lenses

Digital Camera

A digital camera is a photographic device consisting of a lightproof box with a lens at one end, and a digital image sensor at the other in place of the traditional film plane.

There are two basic types of digital cameras -

a. Digital single lens reflex (DSLR)
b. Mirrorless camera

Digital Single-Lens Reflex (DSLR)

This camera is named for the reflexing mirror that allows you to frame the image through the lens prior to capturing the image. As light passes through the DSLR camera's lens, it falls onto a reflexing mirror and then passes through a prism to the viewfinder. The viewfinder image corresponds to the actual image area. When the picture is taken the mirror reflexes, moves up and out of the way, allowing the open shutter to expose the digital image sensor, which captures the image. Most features on a DSLR are adjustable, allowing for greater control over the captured image. DSLR cameras also allow the use of interchangeable lenses, meaning you can swap lenses of different focal lengths on the same camera body.

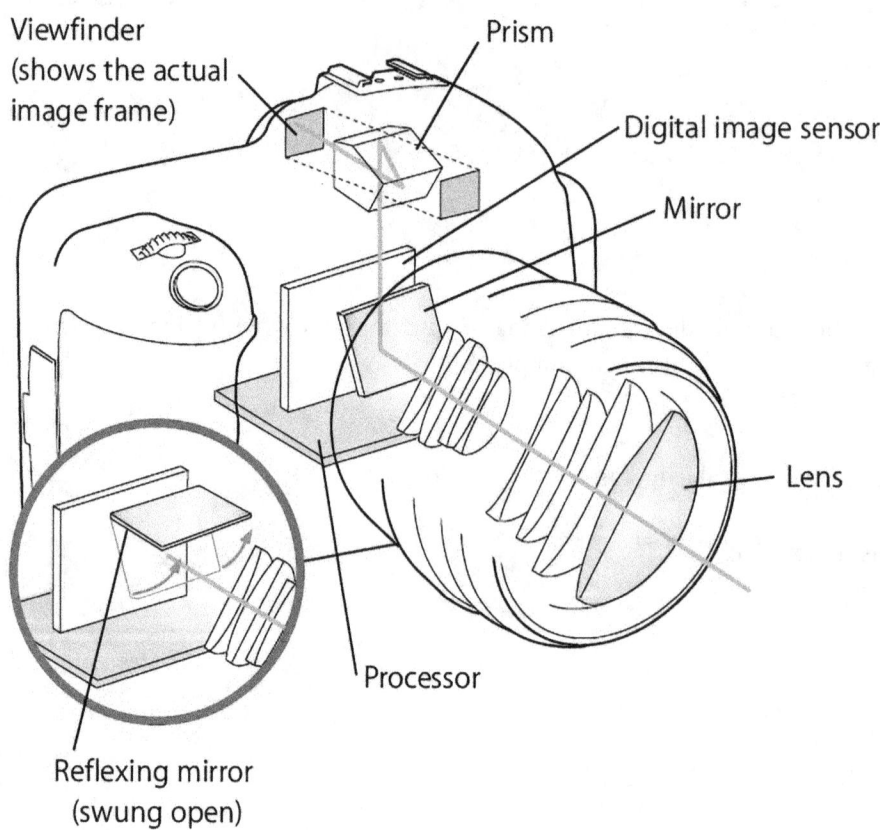

Mirrorless Camera

A Mirrorless camera is a type of camera that works without a reflex mirror. Light passes through the lens directly to the digital sensor, which then displays your image on the camera's LCD screen, allowing you to adjust settings and preview your image before its shot. While previously not considered an interchangeable-lens camera, modifications and advancements have paved the way for more Mirrorless lenses, bringing this camera to the forefront of customizable photography.

The Mirrorless system is more straightforward than the DSLR. Instead of using a mirror to bounce light to the viewfinder and sensor, the sensor is instead directly exposed to light. This generates a live preview of your scene directly to the electronic viewfinder.

When the shutter button is pressed, a door slides up to cover the image sensor. The door will then slide down, exposing the sensor to light. After that, another door slides up to cover the sensor again, which stops exposure, taking the picture.

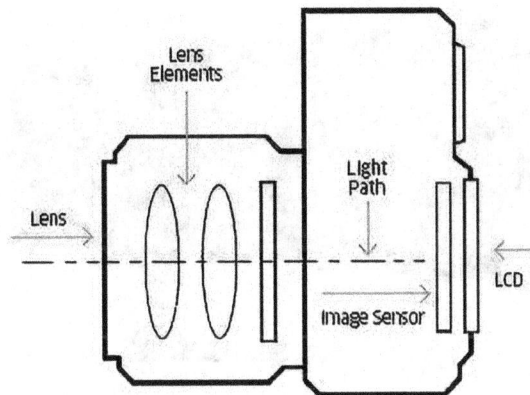

Lens

The lens is a sequence of complicated elements mostly made of glass, built to deflect and focus the light from the subject to the image sensor of a digital camera. Aside from composing the image through your viewfinder, the first contact you have with the light from your subject is through the lens of your camera.

There are several kinds of lenses available to the market but the most basic of these lenses are Telephoto, Wide Angle, Zoom and Prime. They perform the same basic function of the lens: to reflect light from the subject and projects it to the image sensor of the camera.

Telephoto lenses are used to significantly magnify a subject at great distances. A telephoto lens has a long focal distance, meaning that objects closer to the camera will appear slightly out of focus but objects at long range will be clear and precise.

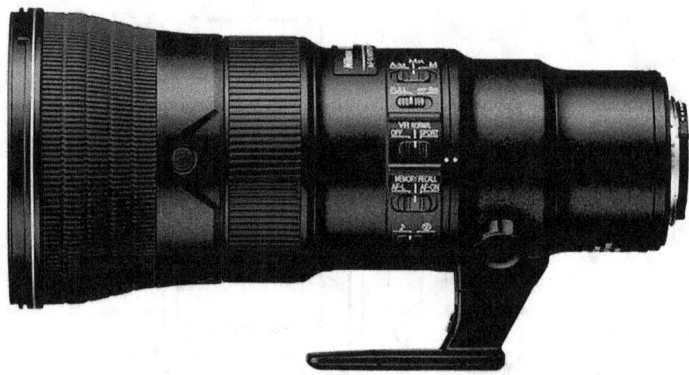

Wide-angle lenses use only a short focal length allowing photographers to concentrate the shot on the main subject but while still get the surrounding area in focus as well.

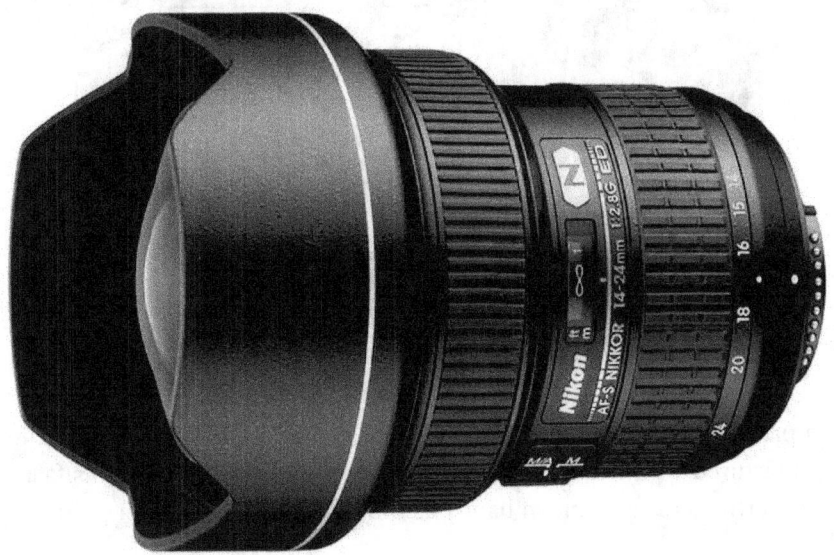

A zoom lens is the type of lens which possesses the mechanical ability to alter its focal length. It is also known as an optical zoom lens. Zoom lenses can provide variable focal lengths to the photographer, making it a productive professional tool. It can alter its focal length from wide angle to standard and from there to zoom.

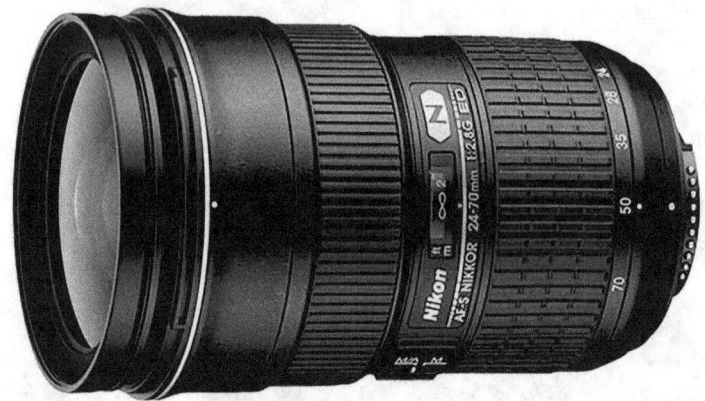

The focal length of a prime lens is unalterable. It is also termed as a fixed lens due to this characteristic. Prime lenses are generally manufactured with wider maximum apertures and the lens speed is faster as a result of that. In darker conditions, wider apertures really come in handy as they can provide brighter pictures.

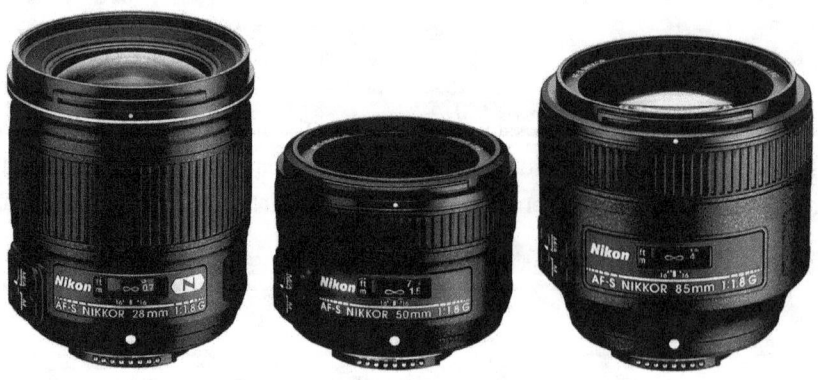

CHAPTER THREE

Common Parts Of Camera

Shutter

The shutter is a device that allows light to pass for a determined period of time, for the purpose of exposing photographic film or a light sensitive electronic sensor to light to capture a permanent image of a scene.

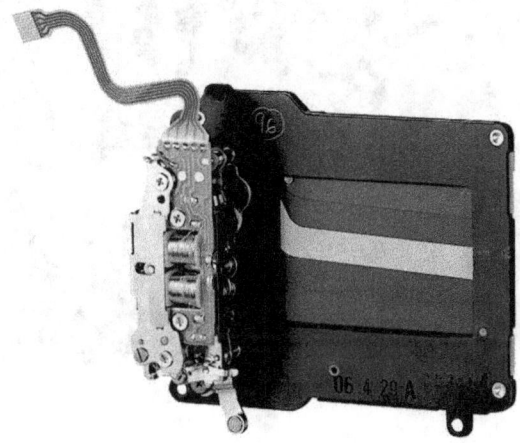

Shutter speed refers to the length of time the shutter is open or the activation of the digital image sensor. The exposure of the photo is produced entirely by the combination of shutter speed and the aperture. Shutter speeds are shown as fractions of a second, such as 1/8 or 1/250. Shutter speed increments are comparable to aperture settings, as each incremental setting either halves or doubles the time of the previous setup. For example, 1/60 of a second is half as much exposure time as 1/30 of a second, and about twice as much as 1/125 of a second.

Image Sensors

There are two kinds of digital image sensors generally used:
   A Charge-coupled device (CCD) and a complementary metal oxide
   Semiconductor (CMOS)

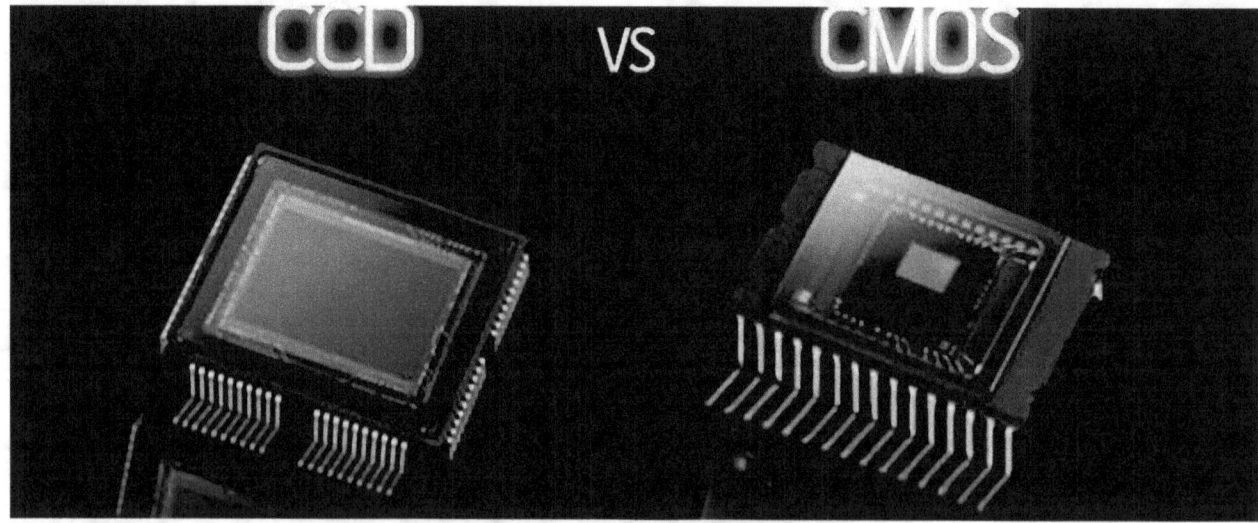

Inbuilt Flash

There are certain photographic situations that need the additionalLight so that the subject could be properly clicked by an internal flash, so that the Built-in flashes could be handy so that they does not required external flash.

Viewfinder

The viewfinder is the small rectangular opening, seen on top of the camera. You can see through this window to compose and frame the shot. Digital cameras either have an optical viewfinder or an electronic viewfinder. The viewfinder also shows parameters like exposure, shutter speed, Aperture, ISO, and a few other basic settings for image capture.

Mode Dial

The Mode dial is another part of a camera used to change different modes. Some of the standard Modes include Aperture mode, Shutter mode, Manual mode and Auto mode.

Hotshoe

Hotshoe is another integral part of a digital camera. It is on the top side of all cameras. It is mainly for mounting the external flash. You can also use it to mount wireless triggers, external microphone, and spirit bubble level. This

Hotshoe mount varies for different camera manufacturers. So, you cannot use one model of external flash on all bodies.

Communication port

Communication ports are usually on either side of the camera. USB is the most common type of communication port, present in all models. It is for image transfer from the camera to the computer. Other communication interfaces include HDMI port, Audio port, Ethernet, Wired remote trigger port, and Display port. These ports may not be present in all models.

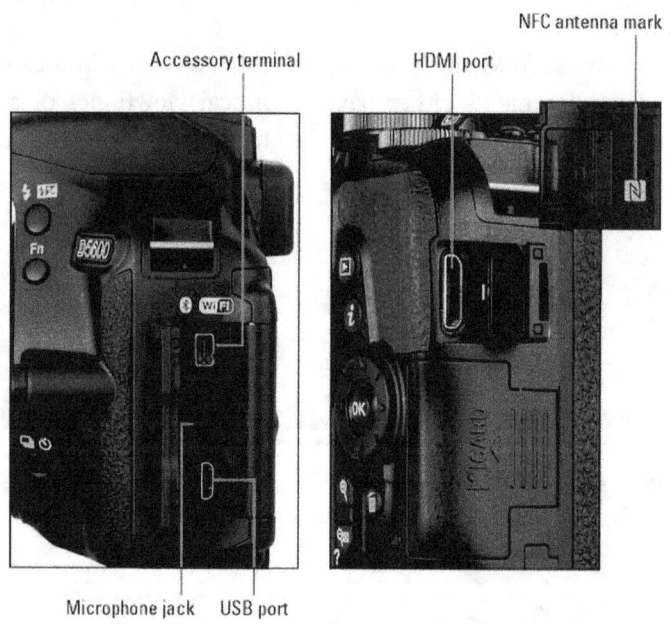

Recording Medium

In digital cameras, the memory card is the photo storage medium. The type of memory card varies with different types of cameras. There will be a card slot located on the side or bottom to insert the memory card. Some cameras come with dual memory card slots.SD card is the commonly supported memory card for most of the digital cameras. Compact Flash card, Micro SD card, XQD card, C Fast card, or some of the other memory cards used in DSLR and Mirrorless digital cameras.

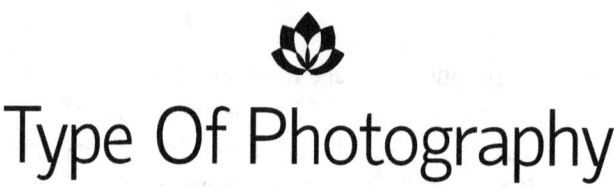

CHAPTER FOUR

Type Of Photography

Type Of Photography

- Nature Photography
- People Photography

Nature Photography

Landscape

Landscape photography can be defined as a photograph taken outdoors in nature. Unlike nature photography however, landscape photography captures an entire scene in nature from an impressive mountain range to a meandering stream through a forest. While man made elements can certainly appear within a landscape photograph, the focus of the image is on the nature in which those elements exist.Landscape photography is a very accessible type of photography, but that doesn't mean it is easy to master.

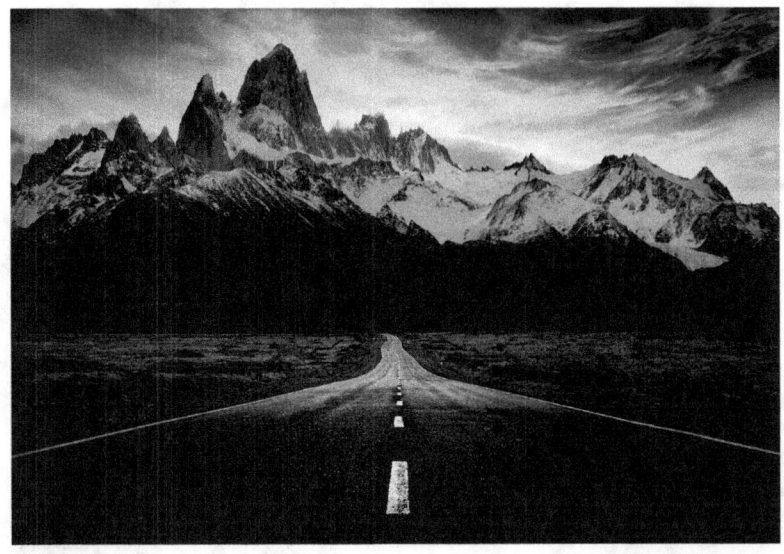

Wildlife

Wildlife photography is a genre of photography concerned with documenting various forms of wildlife in their natural habitat. As well as requiring photography skills, wildlife photographers may need field craft skills. Wildlife photography can bring out some of the most intense photographers you'll meet people who might spend hours on end waiting for an animal to wander into the perfect spot, or search for creatures that most people would rather try to avoid.

But it's also something you can practice in your own backyard, or a short drive from where you live, since there are animals to be found everywhere. From time to time, you'll see a photo series of urban wildlife that rivals the best images captured in more remote locations.

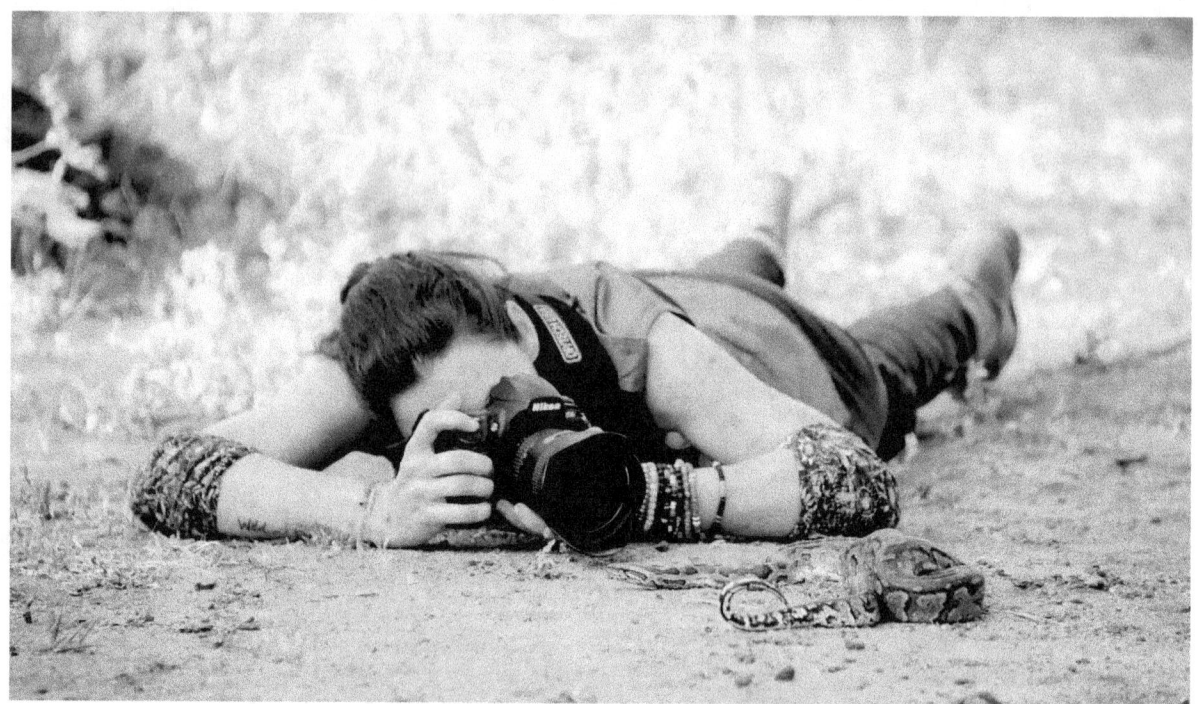

Astrophotography

Astrophotography, also known as astronomical imaging, is photography of astronomical objects, celestial events, and areas of the night sky. The first photograph of an astronomical object was taken in 1840, but it was not until the late 19th century that advances in technology allowed for detailed stellar photography. Astrophotography, both deep-sky and landscapes, have risen in popularity in recent years thanks to the advances of digital camera sensors that have allowed even beginner photographers to get impressive images of the night sky.

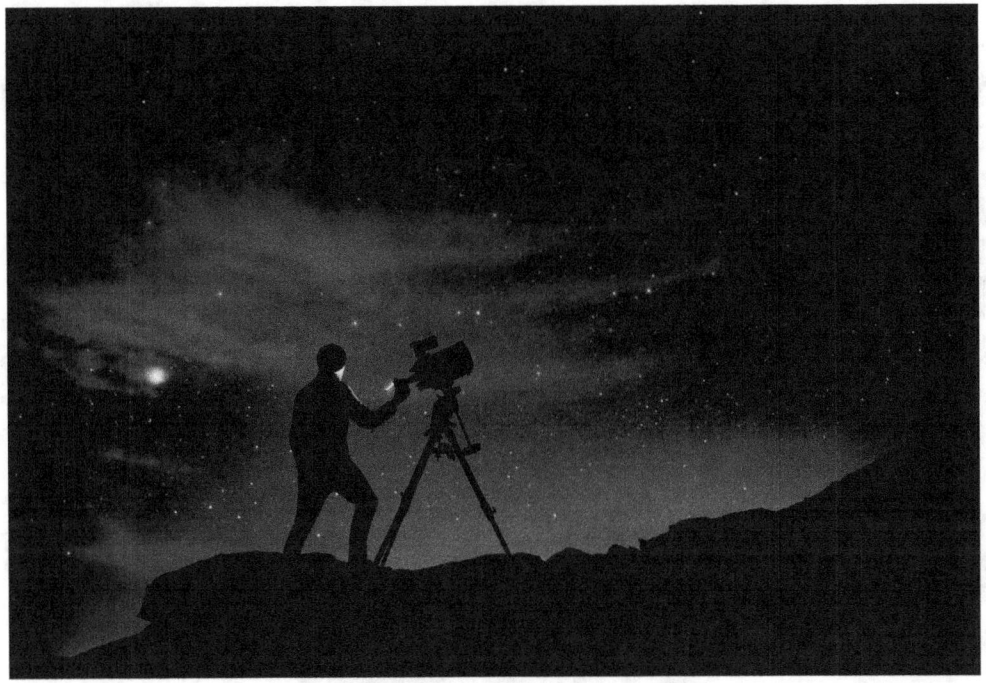

There is also a genre of astrolandscape photography that includes the Milky Way with a slice of Earth in the foreground. Although it is still tricky to take astrolandscape photos, they're a bit easier for most photographers to master.

People Photography

Portraits

The broadest type of people photography is portraiture, covering everything from family portraits to fine-art photography and commercial work. Often, the goal of portraiture is to show the character of a subject to capture the person's personality and emotion in an image. Portrait photography is also quite an accessible genre overall, not requiring more than a single prime lens and flash to start at a high level (or whatever equipment you already have if you're just testing the waters). But capturing the essence of a subject, or meeting the goals for your commercial project, can take a lifetime of work.

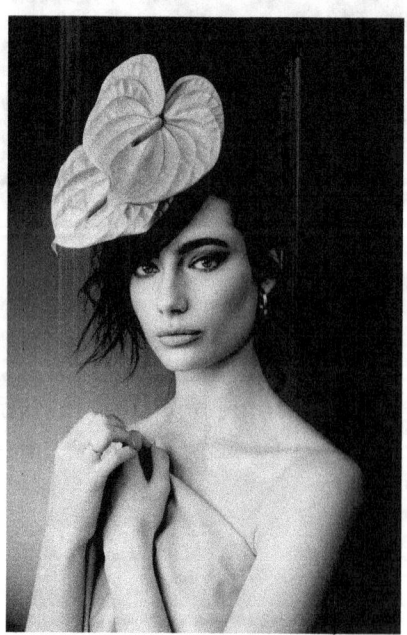

Weddings

One of the most important events in many people's lives is a wedding, and that means wedding photographers have a huge responsibility. Not only do wedding photographers need to have good camera and lighting skills, but they also must know how to work with people and capture the right emotions almost effortlessly. This is a difficult type of photography to practice, and you only get one chance to do it right, so I have a lot of respect for good wedding photographers.

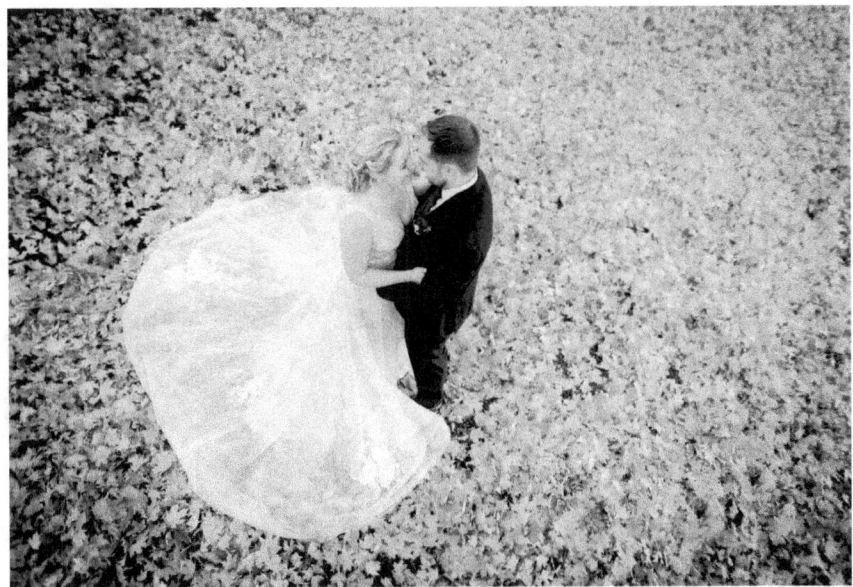

Fashion

A cousin of portraiture, but distinct enough to count as its own genre, is fashion photography. This is a fast-paced world, and the best fashion photographers are intimately knowledgeable not just about lighting and photography but also the clothing styles they are photographing. Fashion photographs are usually intended for brands and advertisements.

There are different types of fashion photography:

- Catalog Photography.
- High Fashion.
- Street Fashion.
- Editorial Fashion

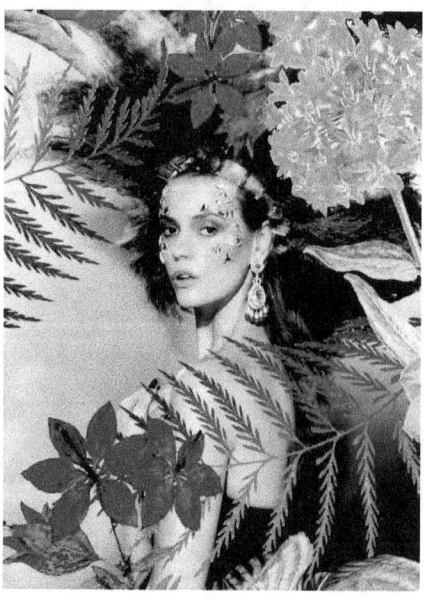

Street Photography

Street photography is about capturing slices of life that happen in common areas in a city, such as parks and sidewalks. Good street photos find meaning and purpose in seemingly ordinary moments or interactions, making viewers think about something they would otherwise pass by. Street photography is often associated with black and white work on 35mm film, but modern-day street photos utilize almost any post-processing styles and camera equipment.

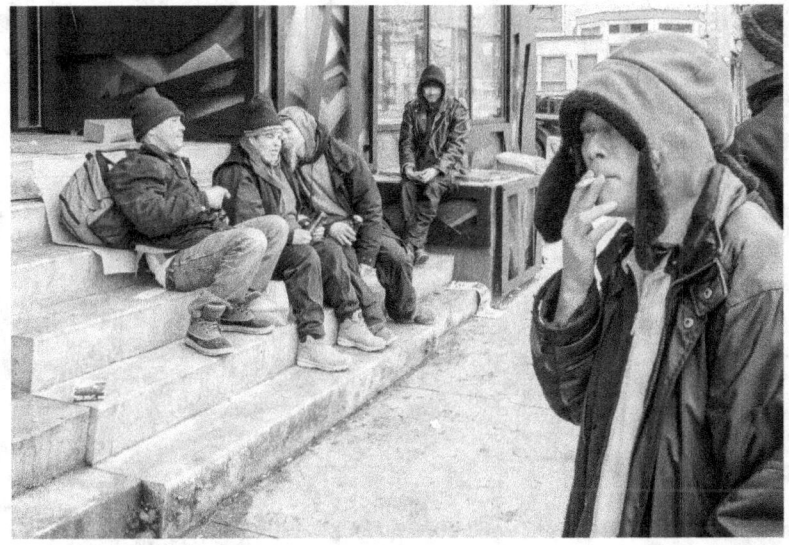

Event Photography

Aside from weddings, there are broader classes of events that deserve recognition as a separate genre of photography. For example, corporate events, concerts, parades, and other celebrations all count as event photography. You can expect unpredictability and fast paced scenes but also interesting human interactions and sometimes (like with concert photos) very good light. Skilled event photographers are able to convey emotions so that viewers are able to relive the moment.

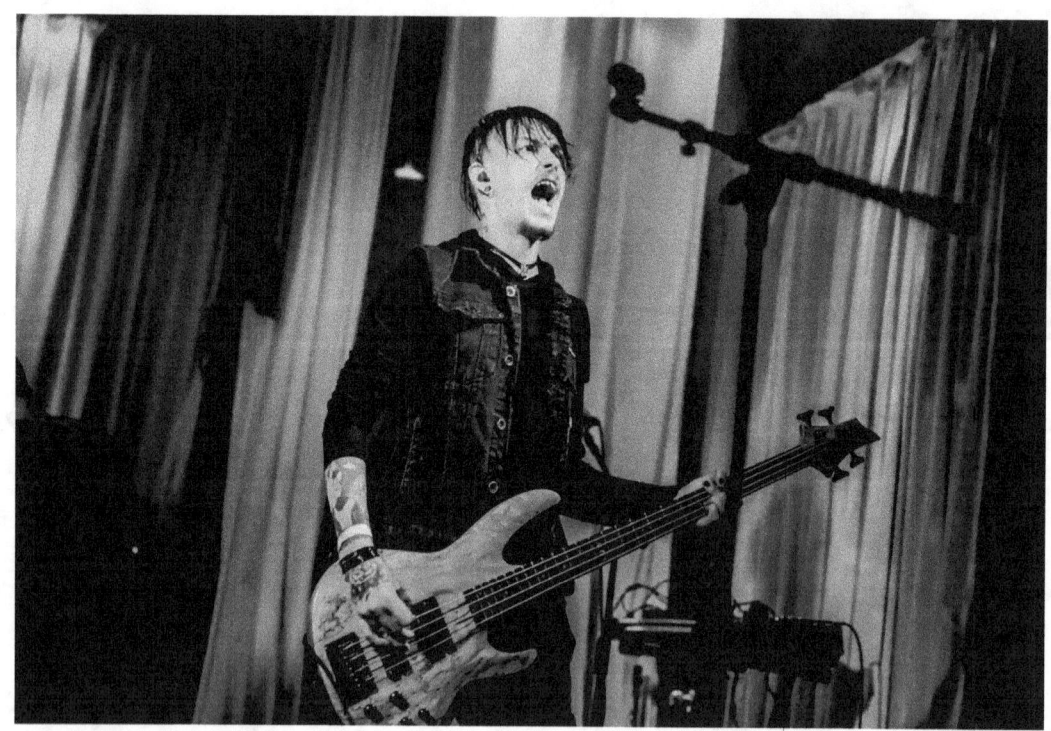

PRONOB NARAYAN DEKA

Other Types Of Photography

Not every photo fits neatly into a single genre of photography. Sometimes, an image will straddle the line between two or more different types, like a landscape image of manmade telescopes under the Milky Way. Is that landscape, architecture, scientific, or astrophotography? It doesn't really matter these genres don't have a hard line between them, and the categories just make it easier to talk about.

Other images might not meet the criteria for any of these categories at all, like surreal composite photography or abstract images where you can't tell what the subject is in the first place. That's perfectly fine, and it doesn't say anything about the quality of a photo one way or another. The point of the list above is to give you some ideas for different styles of photography you may enjoy, not constrict the types of images you can take.

www.ingramcontent.com/pod-product-compliance
Lightning Source LLC
Chambersburg PA
CBHW081246180526
45171CB00005B/557